Beach Cocktails

Beach Cocktails

POURS, DRINKS, SIPS, AND BITES

edited by ALLYSON REEDY

photographs by Lauren McDuffie

Gibbs Smith

First Edition
30 29 28 27 26 5 4 3 2 1

Published by
Gibbs Smith
570 N. Sportsplex Dr.
Kaysville, Utah 84037
www.gibbs-smith.com
The authorized representative in the EEA is Simon and Schuster Netherlands BV, Herculesplein 96 3584 AA Utrecht, Netherlands, info@simonandschuster.nl

Designed by Sheryl Dickert
Production design by Renee Bond
Printed and bound in China

Library of Congress Control Number: 2025938810
ISBN: 978-1-4236-6908-1

This product is made of FSC®-certified and other controlled material.

Contents

Introduction

What makes a cocktail "beach style"? It's more than liking piña coladas and getting caught in the rain. It's more than holding up a tiki mug and bottle of rum and waving in the general direction of the Caribbean. Heck, it's more than the entire catalog of Jimmy Buffett.

Beach drinks are different. They are not the robust, boozy, dark swirls of their speakeasy cousins. They are bright, fruity, and refreshing. They scream out-of-office—a vacation in a glass. Beach drinks are a celebration, a shindig, a tropical jubilee. They're just pure *fun.*

As far as what you'll find in this book, the quick answer is: recipes for beachy drinks like mai tais, margaritas, rum punch, and painkillers, created by iconic bars and resorts, including Death & Co, the Four Seasons, and Max's South Seas Hideaway.

The not-so-quick answer: You'll find recipes that will transport you—mind, body, and spirit—not just to another place, but to a whole other mental state or mood. By performing the almost hallowed ritual of shaking up juices, alcohols, bitters, and ice, you create a divine whole that rises above the sum of its parts.

Besides the tropical drinks (and snacks!) you're expecting, you'll also encounter new favorite cocktails and mocktails, all created by master mixologists who know a thing or two about liquifying adventure and rejuvenation and pouring them into umbrella- and lime-garnished glasses.

And the quickest answer of all: You'll find something really, really good to drink.

The whole point of a beachy drink is to melt your stress away, so lean in to the relaxation and don't stress too much about these recipes. Some mixologists have recommended their favorite spirit brands, but feel free to use whatever brand of rum, tequila, vodka, or fill-in-the-blank spirit you have at home. While you may want to glance over the recipes and pick up some new ingredients for your bar cart the next time you're at the grocery or liquor store, so long as you have a healthy roster of rums and citrus, you're most of the way there.

Of course, part of the appeal of these drinks is the inclusion of tropical fruits, but alas, most of us would be lucky to live within an hour of an international airport, let alone within walking distance of a passion fruit orchard. So yeah, concessions may need to be made. See the

Where to Source Ingredients section (below) for tips on how to score the necessary fruits and purées to nail that Life's a Beach vibe.

Other ditch-the-stress, embrace-the-margarita lifestyle tips: Garnishes are pretty much always optional, and glassware is a suggestion. Your drink will look and feel next level gussied up with an edible orchid and pineapple frond, but guess what? It'll taste just as good without it. Aesthetics are important, yes, but don't let your lack of fresh flora stop you from enjoying a great drink. You're unwinding, remember?

WHO THE RECIPES COME FROM

These drinks are gifted to us from leading mixologists and bartenders who spend their days quenching the thirst of beach-going sun seekers. They know which type of rum goes with what and just how much coconut cream is too much. They shake, blend, and stir for a living, coming from bars, restaurants, and resorts around the world. Nobody knows tropical, tiki, beachy drinks like these folks.

Sometimes these pros note a specific brand they like to use in their recipes, but don't feel constrained to only those bottles. If an ingredient or spirit might be hard to find, I've listed a close substitute, and when exact liquid measurements are left off (i.e., soda water or bubbly for topping), it's because it depends on the glass you're using or your desired concentration.

WHERE TO SOURCE INGREDIENTS

Most of what you need to whip up killer mai tais and frozen chi chis can be found at your local grocery and liquor store. Check the frozen fruit and drink sections for tropical fruits, purées, nectars, and juices, as well as both simple and flavored (like orgeat and coconut) syrups. But to do a few recipes justice might require a bit more looking.

Many fruit purées, like passion and dragon fruit, are available at stores like Walmart and Whole Foods, in addition to international markets, specialty retailers, and online retailers. Dried hibiscus flowers (used for the PYT on page 95) can be found at some grocery stores or at Cost Plus World Market. You can also source it online.

Some recipes from the Infuse Ahead sections require infused spirits or syrups. This may sound difficult, but it's actually about as easy as pouring and waiting. For example, for the jalapeño-infused mezcal for The Pasadena on page 81, the only effort you have to put in is a quick chop of the jalapeños you'll throw into the mezcal. Then, kick back and relax while the peppers do the heavy lifting. It's the same deal with simple syrup, where you're boiling sugar, water, and whatever ingredient is going to punch up your drink.

SIMPLE SYRUP

Here's a basic simple syrup recipe, but to jazz it up with flavors like cinnamon or passion fruit, all you do is add the bonus ingredient to the pan. See? It's called simple *syrup for a reason.*

MAKES 1½ CUPS; 1:1 SUGAR TO WATER RATIO

1 cup water
1 cup sugar

Combine the sugar and the water in a medium saucepan over medium heat. Bring to a boil and stir until the sugar fully dissolves. Remove from the heat and allow to cool for 15 minutes. Pour into a sterilized jar, add the lid, label, and store for up to 1 month in the refrigerator.

FOR CINNAMON SYRUP: Add 3 cinnamon sticks with the water and sugar. Boil, strain, and store as directed.

FOR GUAVA SYRUP: Stir in 1 cup guava puree with the water and sugar. Boil, strain, and store as directed.

FOR GINGER SYRUP: Add ¾ cup sliced and peeled ginger root with the water and sugar. Boil, strain, and store as directed.

FOR PASSION FRUIT SYRUP: Stir 1 cup passion fruit pulp into 1 cup fresh simple syrup. Strain and store as directed.

FOR COCONUT SYRUP: Stir in 1 teaspoon coconut extract with the water and sugar. Boil, strain, and store as directed.

FOR DEMERARA SYRUP: Swap demerara sugar for white sugar. Boil, strain, and store as directed.

FOR HONEY SYRUP: Swap honey for white sugar. Boil, cool, and store as directed.

SALINE SOLUTION

A few recipes call for saline solution, which is as easy as stirring salt into water.

MAKES ⅓ CUP

⅓ cup (80 grams) hot water
1 tablespoon (20 grams) kosher salt

Pour the water and salt into a jar and stir until salt is dissolved. Allow it to sit for a few minutes until the mixture is clear. Pour mixture into a dropper bottle and store in a cool, dark place.

EQUIPMENT YOU'LL NEED

Besides the liquid ingredients, there are just a few more things you need to get going on your tropical cocktail adventure. While heavy packers can also load up their bar carts with fancy ice molds, peelers, and siphons, this list is for those who prefer to travel light.

Blender

For frozen drinks, you'll need a blender to pulverize the ice and make it nice and frosty.

Citrus Juicer

Especially for beachy drinks using fresh fruit, a handheld juicer is handy.

Fine-Mesh Strainer

This is used for straining ice and other solids out of drinks before you pour them into the glass. It is also helpful when making simple syrups and spirit infusions.

Glasses

You need something to hold that delicious cocktail you just shook up. Practically speaking, any glass will do, but it's scientifically proven that drinks taste better when sipped out of cool cups. The cocktails and mocktails in this book utilize all sorts of glasses, including tiki mugs, rocks, collins, coupes, martinis, and hurricanes.

Ice

The unsung hero of cocktails and mocktails! Used for blending, shaking, mixing, and cooling, ice is critical. You can get by with standard-sized cubes, you can use crushed or pebble, or you can kick it up a notch with giant cubes and spheres. Remember, the smaller the cube, the faster it melts, thus diluting the drink.

Jigger/Measuring Glass

A jigger is a two-sided measuring tool for pouring liquor. You can also use a shot glass or other measuring glass that denotes ounces.

Muddler

Some drinks, like the mojito, require herbs or fruit to be smashed to get their essence into the drink. If you don't have a dedicated muddler, you can also use the back of a wooden spoon.

Shaker

There are different types of shaking devices out there, including the Boston (with a metal shaking tin and glass mixing tin), the Parisian (both shaking and mixing tins are metal), and the Cobbler (the one you likely have at home with a metal shaking tin, lid with built-in holes for straining, and a cap). So long as you've got one of these, you're good to go.

Stir Stick/Bar Spoon

Basically, any long-handled, narrow device that can stir up your drink works.

And finally, what are you waiting for? It's five o'clock somewhere. . . .

RUM-BASED COCKTAILS: SHAKE & SIP

"The best ideas come while sipping rum."

—Pavol Kazimir

OCTOPUS OASIS

AURORA ANGUILLA RESORT & GOLF CLUB

Rum is sort of synonymous with beach drinks—the sugarcane-based spirit originated in the Caribbean, and it became the drink of choice for sailors everywhere. (Yo, ho, ho, anyone?) Named for the super cool creatures found swimming off the coast of the Caribbean Island of Anguilla, this drink is a trio of rums, along with sweet, nutty orgeat and tangy lime for a well-balanced cocktail that somehow tastes even better with an umbrella in it.

SERVES 1

1 ounce Bacardí Superior rum, or other light rum
1 ounce Malibu coconut rum, or other coconut rum
1 ounce Goslings Black Seal rum, or other dark rum
1 ounce orgeat syrup
1 ounce lime juice
3 dashes Angostura bitters
Lime wheel, for garnish
Mint sprig, for garnish

GLASS: tiki or rocks

Add rums, orgeat syrup, lime juice, and Angostura bitters to a shaker filled with ice. Shake well for a couple of seconds. Strain the mixture into your glass of choice filled with ice. Garnish with a lime wheel, mint sprig, or any other tropical flair.

GUMBY SLUMBER

LITTLE PALM ISLAND RESORT & SPA, LITTLE TORCH KEY, FL

The best part of this fruity, rummy signature cocktail at Little Palm Island Resort & Spa? The equal ratios of everything make it super easy to scale up for a bigger group. Or keep it as-is if you'd prefer to dream of the Keys solo.

SERVES 1

1 ounce Captain Morgan spiced rum, or other spiced rum
1 ounce Parrot Bay coconut rum, or other coconut rum
1 ounce pineapple juice
1 ounce cranberry juice
1 ounce orange juice
Fresh coconut, for garnish (optional)

GLASS: hurricane or rocks

Combine rums with juices in a mixing glass and mix well. Serve chilled in your glass of choice filled with ice, and garnish with fresh coconut. If using the coconut garnish, try marinating in an overproof rum.

LITTLE PALM-ARITA

LITTLE PALM ISLAND RESORT & SPA, LITTLE TORCH KEY, FL

Like a margarita, but a little coconut-y and vanilla-y, this cocktail is easy to whip up, and even easier to drink. Having one in hand on the beach—or while pretending you're on the beach—is a must.

SERVES 1

1½ ounces Flecha Azul blanco tequila, or other blanco tequila
1½ ounces Malibu coconut rum, or other coconut rum
1 ounce Licor 43
1 ounce agave nectar
Fresh coconut shavings, for garnish
Pineapple slice, for garnish (optional)

GLASS: collins or preferred glass

In a shaker filled with ice, combine tequila, rum, Licor 43, and agave. Shake and strain into a collins glass or glass of choice filled with fresh ice. Garnish with fresh coconut shavings and a pineapple slice, if using.

KENDIE'S KICK RUM PUNCH

KENDIE WILLIAMS, FOUR SEASONS RESORT NEVIS, ST. KITTS AND NEVIS

Generally, master mixologist Kendie Williams would be the first to tell you that a light rum is best for rum punch, but for her signature recipe, she made an exception. The spiced rum gives her punch a complex kick, and it works beautifully with the tart tamarind and passion fruit purées. (Kendie plucks the fruit from her garden, but store-bought is fine if you don't, you know, live on an idyllic tropical island.)

SERVES 1

2 ounces Crowned Monkey rum, or other spiced rum
1 ounce Brinley vanilla rum, or other vanilla rum
1½ ounces passion fruit purée
1 ounce tamarind purée, or tamarind juice or nectar
½ ounce lime juice
1 dash Angostura bitters
Lime wedge, for garnish
Grated nutmeg, for garnish

GLASS: rocks

Pour rums, purées, lime juice, and bitters into a shaker with ice and give it a good shake. Strain into a rocks glass filled with ice. Garnish with a lime wedge and grated nutmeg.

SKY HIGH MOJITO

PRINCESS HOTELS & RESORTS, JAMAICA

What happens when a classic mojito gets a jolt of coconut? This delicious twist, which tastes like paradise in every sip. It's one of the signature cocktails at Princess Hotels & Resorts, Jamaica and will probably become one of yours, too.

SERVES 1

5 lime wedges
Handful of mint
1½ ounces Appleton white rum, or other white rum
1 ounce coconut rum
1 ounce Simple Syrup (page 10)
Plain sparkling soda water or club soda
Drizzle of blue Curaçao

GLASS: collins

Begin by muddling lime wedges and mint in a cocktail shaker to release their aromatic essence. Add ice, rums, and simple syrup to the shaker, then shake gently to combine. Strain the mixture into a collins glass, top with sparkling soda water, and finish with a delicate drizzle of blue Curaçao.

THE EYE OF THE STORM

ANGEL HORTA LUPIAC, KIMPTON SURFCOMBER HOTEL, MIAMI, FL

Don't be scared off by the foreboding name—this cocktail shakes up strawberries, passion fruit, and lime juice with white rum, and yes, it tastes just as good as you're imagining. Perfect for sunny, stormy, and everything-in-between weather.

SERVES 1

1½ ounces Bacardí Superior blanco rum, or other white rum
1 ounce strawberry purée
½ ounce passion fruit purée
¼ ounce lime juice
Lime slice, for garnish (optional)

GLASS: rocks

Pour rum, purées, and lime juice into a shaker filled with ice. Give it a good shake and strain into a rocks glass over ice. Garnish with a slice of lime, if using.

Dark & Stormy

DARK & STORMY

ROSEWOOD BERMUDA

The national drink of Bermuda got its name from its appearance, looking like a dark, stormy cloud no one would want to sail under. Luckily, you don't have to sail under this cloud of ginger beer and dark rum, only drink it. There are only two ingredients, so make sure you're using the good stuff.

SERVES 1

4 ounces Barritt's ginger beer, or other ginger beer
2 ounces Goslings Black Seal rum, or other dark rum
Lime slice, for garnish

GLASS: highball

Fill glass with ice and pour in ginger beer. Top with rum and garnish with lime.

BAJAN BUS STOP

TROY DELORT, HILTON BARBADOS RESORT

Showcasing a range of Barbados's stellar libations, this drink is definitely transporting you to the Caribbean. While it's intended to be made with all Barbadian products (shoutout to Banks beer), you can recreate it with closer-to-home substitutes if you can't score the mauby syrup and Banks.

SERVES 1

1½ ounces Mount Gay XO rum, or other aged rum
1 ounce falernum
1 ounce mauby syrup, or blackstrap molasses syrup
3 ounces Banks beer, or other pilsner lager
Salt

GLASS: pilsner

Pour rum, falernum, and mauby syrup into a shaker filled with ice. Strain into pilsner glass, top with beer, and sprinkle a little salt on top.

SILVERSANDS TROPICAL BLISS

SILVERSANDS RESORT GRENADA AT GRAND ANSE

There's no denying the dynamic duo that is passion fruit and coconut cream. They go together like a tropical peanut butter and jelly, a beachy Batman and Robin. Add some rum, lime, simple syrup, and bitters to the classic combo, and you'll understand why they call this one bliss.

SERVES 1

1½ ounces premium white rum
¾ ounce lime juice
¾ ounce passion fruit purée
½ ounce coconut cream
¼ ounce Simple Syrup (page 10)
1 dash Angostura bitters
Pineapple slice, for garnish
Mint sprig, for garnish

GLASS: chilled hurricane or highball

In a cocktail shaker, combine rum, lime juice, passion fruit purée, coconut cream, simple syrup, and bitters. Fill the shaker with crushed ice and shake vigorously until well chilled. Strain the mixture into a chilled glass of your choice filled with crushed ice. Garnish with pineapple slice and mint sprig.

GHOST OF CHRISTMAS PASSED OUT

HYATT REGENCY HUNTINGTON BEACH, CA

This take on the mai tai is served in the most festive and merriest holiday pop-up bar: Hyatt Regency Huntington Beach's annual Pete's Christmas Vacation. The bar is part winter wonderland, part tropical paradise, but this drink is all sweet, nutty, rum perfection.

SERVES 1

1¼ ounces Ten To One white rum, or other white rum
1¼ ounces Mount Gay Black Barrel rum, or other aged rum
¾ ounce orgeat syrup
¾ ounce Cointreau
2 ounces mai tai mix
¾ ounce lime juice
Pineapple frond, for garnish
Orchid, for garnish (optional)

GLASS: tiki mug

Pour the rums, orgeat syrup, Cointreau, mai tai mix, and lime juice into a shaker filled with ice. Give it a good shake and then strain into a tiki mug filled with fresh ice. Garnish with pineapple frond and orchid, if using.

LOVANGO RUM PUNCH

LOVANGO RESORT & BEACH CLUB, U. S. VIRGIN ISLANDS

There are probably as many versions of rum punch as there are islands in the Caribbean, and just like all those sunny isles, you'll probably want to get acquainted with them all. Lovango's sweet, spiced take on the quintessential punch is as tasty of a start as any.

SERVES 1

1½ ounces Plantation 3 Stars white rum, or other white rum
½ ounce Little Gem Spirits sweet tamarind rum, or previous white rum
1 ounce falernum
2 ounces pineapple juice
1 ounce lime juice
1 ounce grenadine
Pineapple fronds, for garnish
Pineapple slice, for garnish

GLASS: hurricane

Pour rums, falernum, pineapple juice, lime juice, and grenadine into a shaker filled with ice. Shake hard for 10 seconds and strain over fresh ice in a hurricane glass. Top with pebble ice and garnish with pineapple fronds and slice.

JUMP UP JUICE

BASIL'S BAR, MUSTIQUE ISLAND, ST. VINCENT AND THE GRENADINES

This one will definitely get you jumping. The strong blend of spirits is only mildly tempered with gusts of lime and simple syrup. It's bold, boozy, and delicious no matter the weather.

SERVES 1

1 ounce strong white rum
1 ounce dark rum
1 ounce vodka
½ ounce Kahlúa, or other coffee liqueur
½ ounce lime juice
½ ounce Simple Syrup (page 10)
Lime wedge, for garnish

GLASS: rocks

Combine rums, vodka, coffee liqueur, lime juice, and simple syrup in a shaker filled with ice. Shake hard and strain into a rocks glass with ice. Garnish with lime.

ANGUILLITA

ALTAMER LUXURY VILLAS, ANGUILLA

Yes, you could jet off to Anguilla to try this coconutty, gingery cocktail for yourself—and yeah, it probably does taste even better on Altamer's scenic stretch of beach—but it's a whole lot faster and cheaper to try it at home. To squeeze the ginger, you can use a juicer, blender, garlic press, or plain-old cheesecloth. Have fun with garnishes and try a slice of dragon fruit and lime slices for additional color.

SERVES 1

1 ounce Myers's rum, or other dark rum
4 ounces coconut water
½ ounce ginger juice
½ ounce lime juice
½ ounce guava purée

GLASS: rocks

Pour rum, coconut water, juices, and guava purée into a mixing glass or shaker filled with ice. Give it a good shake and strain into a rocks glass with ice.

CIDER SUNSET

THE SOMERSET ON GRACE BAY, TURKS AND CAICOS

Take your favorite cider to the tropics with the addition of spiced rum and citrus. A sprinkling of cinnamon makes it smell amazing and gives it a little kick.

SERVES 1

1 ounce spiced rum
1 ounce orange juice
Dash of cinnamon
4 ounces Somerset cider, or other semi-sweet cider
Orange slice, for garnish (optional)
Cinnamon stick, for garnish (optional)

GLASS: highball

In a shaker filled with ice, combine rum, orange juice, and cinnamon. Shake well and strain into a highball glass filled with ice. Top with cider and stir gently to combine. Garnish with orange slice and/or cinnamon stick.

CURTAIN CALL

SUMMER GOFF, DEATH & CO, DENVER, CO

This gutsy drink is made for the very, very spirited. After all, it combines the highest of high-proof rums with another rum, amaro, and *coffee liqueur. Luckily there's also pineapple and orange juices, plus coconut cream, to balance the buzz.*

SERVES 1

1 ounce Denizen Vatted dark rum, or other dark rum
½ ounce Lemon Hart 151, or other high-proof rum
½ ounce Mr Black cold brew coffee liqueur, or other coffee liqueur
½ ounce Amaro Averna, or other amaro
¾ ounce pineapple juice
¾ ounce orange juice
¾ ounce Coco Lopez, or other coconut cream
Mint, for garnish
Orange slice, for garnish
Grated coffee bean, for garnish (optional)

GLASS: tulip

Pour rums, coffee liqueur, amaro, pineapple juice, orange juice, and coconut cream into a shaker with 12 or so pieces of pebble ice. Whip shake it, or shake until the ice melts. Strain into a tulip glass filled with pebble ice, and garnish with mint, orange slice, and grated coffee bean, if using.

SPIRIT OF ALOHA

ROYAL LAHAINA RESORT & BUNGALOWS, MAUI, HI

Ube is a staple in Hawaii; the purple root vegetable offers a mildly sweet and nutty flavor as well as a showstopping hue. Here, ube syrup is balanced with coconut rum and lime and pineapple juices for a drink that screams aloha.

SERVES 1

2 ounces Kōloa Kauaʻi coconut rum, or other coconut rum
2 ounces ube syrup
1 ounce lime juice
½ ounce Coconut Syrup (page 10)
½ ounce pineapple juice
Lime slice, for garnish (optional)
Pineapple slice, for garnish (optional)

GLASS: snifter

Pour coconut rum, ube syrup, lime juice, coconut syrup, and pineapple juice in a shaker filled with ice. Give it a good shake and strain into a snifter glass filled with fresh ice. Garnish with lime and pineapple, if using.

RUM-BASED COCKTAILS: INFUSE AHEAD

"All roads lead to rum."

—W. C. Fields

THE LOVE BOAT

MATT GRIMES, SWAYLO'S TIKI, LONGMONT, CO

Yes, the ingredient list might look a little long, but this could quite possibly be the ideal tropical sip. And when ideal tropical sips are involved, what's a little orgeat syrup and overproof rum? The syrups are as easy to make as boiling water, and all the ingredients are readily available. You know what to do.

SERVES 1

1¼ ounces Rittenhouse rye whiskey, or other rye whiskey
1¼ ounces The Real McCoy 3 year aged rum, or other aged silver rum
1 ounce Planteray O.F.T.D. overproof rum, or other overproof rum
2 ounces pineapple juice
1½ ounces lemon juice
1 ounce Cinnamon Syrup (page 10)
½ ounce Orgeat Syrup (below)
4 dashes Bittercube ginger allspice bitters, or other aromatic bitters
Edible orchids, for garnish
Lime wheels, for garnish

GLASS: tiki mug

Add all ingredients, except for garnishes, into a shaker. Add a scoop of ice and shake for 10 seconds. Dump ice and drink into your favorite tiki mug and garnish with orchids and limes.

Orgeat Syrup

MAKES 2 CUPS

1 cup almond milk
¾ cup sugar
½ cup water
¼ teaspoon almond extract

Add all ingredients into a large pot and bring to a boil over high heat. Reduce for 10 minutes and ensure sugar is dissolved. Remove from heat and allow mixture to cool before use.

VANILLAKILLA

MATT GRIMES, SWAYLO'S TIKI, LONGMONT, CO

Warning: the Vanillakilla is so smoothly delicious that you might forget there's alcohol in there. The coconut cream adds richness to the pineapple and orange juices, and the freshly grated nutmeg on top takes it to the next level of tropical sipping bliss.

SERVES 1

2 ounces Vanilla Bean-Infused Rum (below)
4 ounces pineapple juice
1 ounce coconut cream
1 ounce orange juice
Freshly grated nutmeg, for garnish
Pineapple fronds, for garnish

GLASS: large snifter or preferred glass

Add vanilla bean-infused rum, pineapple juice, coconut cream, and orange juice to a shaker filled with a scoop of ice. Shake for 10 seconds and dump contents into a large snifter or preferred glass filled with fresh ice. Garnish with a healthy amount of freshly grated nutmeg and pineapple fronds.

Vanilla Bean–Infused Rum

MAKES ONE 750-MILLILITER BOTTLE

1 (750-milliliter) bottle Planteray Original dark rum, or other dark rum
1 whole vanilla bean

Cut the vanilla bean lengthwise and scrape the seeds out. Add bean and seeds directly into the rum bottle. Allow to sit at least overnight, but the longer it infuses, the better it gets.

BOG CUTTER

JAKE POWELL, DEATH & CO, DENVER, CO

This drink has more layers than a wedding cake. You get notes of lemon's bright citrus, orgeat's creamy almond, amaro's bittersweet herbs, cinnamon syrup's spicy kick, and banana's tropical smoothness. (And we haven't even gotten to the boozy rums and gin.) The complexity of this drink unfolds with every sip.

SERVES 1

1½ ounces Denizen Vatted dark rum, or other dark rum
¼ ounce Wray & Nephew rum, or other Jamaican rum
½ ounce Amaro Averna, or other amaro
½ ounce orgeat syrup
¼ ounce Four Pillars navy strength gin, or other navy strength gin
¼ ounce Tempus Fugit Crème de Banane, or other banana liqueur
1 ounce lemon juice
¼ ounce Cinnamon Syrup (page 10)
Mint sprig, for garnish (optional)
Edible orchid, for garnish (optional)
Cinnamon, freshly grated, for garnish (optional)

GLASS: tulip

Pour rums, amaro, orgeat syrup, gin, banana liqueur, lemon juice, and cinnamon syrup into a shaker with 12 or so pieces of pebble ice. Whip shake it, or shake until the ice melts. Strain into a tulip glass filled with pebble ice and garnish with mint, orchid, and grated cinnamon, if using.

DARK SEA SCOUNDREL

SEAN BIGGS, SHIPWRECKED TIKI BAR, DAVIS, CA

Shipwrecked Tiki Bar has its own scale for measuring the booziness of its cocktails, and the spiced Dark Sea Scoundrel falls between balanced and pirate strength, so yes, it's going to pack a punch. To really ace the presentation, singe a cinnamon stick with a kitchen torch or your stove. (Don't worry; it's a slow burn and shouldn't set your house ablaze.)

SERVES 1

¾ ounce Planteray O.F.T.D. overproof rum, or other overproof rum
¾ ounce dark cacao liqueur
½ ounce horchata cream liqueur
½ ounce lime juice
½ ounce Bourbon Spice Simple Syrup (below)
2 dashes orange bitters
2 dashes Saline Solution (page 11)
Pineapple frond, for garnish
Dehydrated lime wheel, for garnish
Smoldering cinnamon stick, for garnish

GLASS: old fashioned

Pour rum, liqueurs, lime juice, simple syrup, bitters, and saline in a Boston shaker filled with ice. Give it a good shake and strain into glass with fresh ice. Garnish with pineapple frond, lime wheel, and cinnamon stick.

Bourbon Spice Simple Syrup

MAKES ABOUT 2 CUPS

1 cup water
1 cup cane sugar
½ cup demerara sugar, or turbinado or raw sugar
½ teaspoon ground cinnamon
⅛ teaspoon ground nutmeg
2 tablespoons bourbon
1 teaspoon vanilla extract

In a medium saucepan over medium-low heat, whisk water, sugars, cinnamon, and nutmeg until dissolved. Bring to a boil, then remove from heat. Pour into a large mason jar or other airtight container, cover, and let sit for 10 minutes. Add bourbon and vanilla, and use once it's cool. Store in refrigerator for up to 2 weeks.

STEP PAPI

RICKY RAMIREZ, THE MOTHERSHIP, MILWAUKEE, WI

No matter what's going on in your home right now—leaky pipes, a cat vomiting, kids fighting with golf clubs—this drink will make it all slightly more pleasant, or as pleasant as leaky pipes, sick cats, and warring kids can be made. The sweet and bitter of the passion fruit and aperitivo play really well together (unlike your children), and the overproof rum gives it the kick in the pants you (and they) need.

SERVES 1

1 ounce Wray & Nephew rum, or other unaged overproof Jamaican rum
¾ ounce sloe gin
½ ounce bitter aperitivo blend (equal parts Campari and wine-based red bitter)
⅓ ounce orgeat syrup
3 dashes absinthe
¾ ounce Passion Fruit Syrup (page 10)
½ ounce lime juice
3 dashes Angostura bitters

GLASS: pilsner

Pour all ingredients into a shaker with crushed ice. Give it a good shake and dump everything into a pilsner glass.

TIKI TEPACHE

ALEX VALENCIA, LA CONTENTA LES AND VALLARTA TROPICAL, NEW YORK, NY

If you don't yet know tepache, you're about to be hooked. It's a traditional Mexican fermented drink made from pineapple rinds, spices, and sugar. Inspired by Mexico's 1950s tiki bar scene, you know this drink is going to be a glass of good vibes. Just make sure you plan ahead, as the tepache takes a few days to ferment.

SERVES 1

1½ ounces rhum agricole
½ ounce Curaçao
¾ ounce lime juice
¾ ounce Demerara Syrup (page 10)
3 dashes of Angostura bitters
3 ounces Sazón Tepache (below)
Pineapple leaves, for garnish (optional)
Pineapple slice, for garnish
Ground cinnamon, for garnish

GLASS: tiki mug

Add rhum agricole, Curaçao, lime juice, demerara syrup, and bitters to a shaker. Add 2 ice cubes and shake. Pour into a tiki mug filled with pebble or crushed ice. Last, add the 3 ounces of sazón tepache on top. Garnish with a couple pineapple leaves, if using, a slice of pineapple, and sprinkle a little cinnamon on top.

Sazón Tepache

MAKES ABOUT 1 GALLON

1 organic pineapple, peeled and chopped (use just the rind and core, saving the fruit for another use)
1 cup piloncillo, or brown sugar
1 gallon water
1 cinnamon stick
2 to 3 whole cloves

In a large pot, combine all ingredients. Bring to a boil, then reduce heat and simmer for 30 minutes. Remove from heat and let steep for 2 to 3 hours or overnight.

Strain the liquid through a cheesecloth or fine-mesh sieve into a large container. Discard solids and reserve liquid. Transfer liquid to a glass jar or container with a wide mouth. Cover with cloth or paper towel, securing with rubber band. Let ferment at room temperature (68 to 72°F) for 2 to 3 days, or until bubbles appear. Stir daily to prevent mold.

After 2 to 3 days, strain the liquid through a fine-mesh sieve into a clean container. It's ready for drinking or to be mixed into cocktails. Store in the refrigerator for up to a week, but it is best if consumed within a few days.

IM-PECK-ABLE DAIQUIRI

CORWYN CAMPOS, THE BIRDCAGE, HOTEL WAILEA, MAUI, HI

To Maui-fy the classic daiquiri, the Hotel Wailea uses—what else?—pineapple juice. They adjust the acid levels to mimic lime's tartness, giving the drink Hawaiian flair without sacrificing the ideal balance of sweet and tart.

SERVES 1

1 ounce Kuleana Nanea rum, or other dry Caribbean rum
½ ounce KōHana KEA agricole rum, or other white rum
½ ounce Smith & Cross navy strength rum, or other navy strength rum
¾ ounce Sugar Cane Dane Maui cane syrup, or Simple Syrup (page 10)
¾ ounce Acid-Adjusted Pineapple Juice (below)
Dehydrated or fresh pineapple half-moon, for garnish (optional)
Edible dianthus flower, for garnish (optional)

GLASS: coupe

Combine rums, syrup, and pineapple juice in a Boston shaker filled with ice and shake vigorously for approximately 10 seconds. Strain the cocktail back into the small tin and remove the ice from the large tin. Shake vigorously again for approximately 10 seconds. This secondary shake will develop a frothy head because of the pineapple juice. Strain into a coupe glass and garnish with a dehydrated pineapple half-moon rested on the rim with an edible dianthus flower on top, if using.

Acid-Adjusted Pineapple Juice

MAKES ABOUT 3 OUNCES

100 milliliters pineapple juice
3.2 grams citric acid
2 grams malic acid

Stir acids into the pineapple juice until they dissolve. Store in a mason jar or other airtight container in the refrigerator for up to a week.

MOTHERSHIP BLUE HAWAIIAN

RICKY RAMIREZ, THE MOTHERSHIP, MILWAUKEE, WI

The Blue Hawaiian was created in Waikiki in the 1950s, but it tastes just as fresh in your kitchen right now. Sort of like a blue piña colada, The Mothership's version adds passion fruit liqueur and a few dashes of cinnamon tincture for an added warm tanginess. The cinnamon tincture takes a couple days to infuse, so I like to make up a batch to have on-hand.

SERVES 1

2 ounces Probitas rum, or preferred white rum
½ ounce Chinola passion fruit liqueur, or other passion fruit liqueur
¼ ounce Combier blue Curaçao, or other blue Curaçao
1½ ounces pineapple juice
1 ounce Coco Lopez, or other coconut cream
½ ounce lemon juice
3 dashes Cinnamon Tincture (below)

GLASS: double old fashioned

Pour rum, passion fruit liqueur, blue Curaçao, pineapple juice, coconut cream, lemon juice, and cinnamon tincture into a shaker filled with crushed ice. Give it a good shake and dump into a double old-fashioned glass. Add more crushed ice.

Cinnamon Tincture

MAKES 6 OUNCES

2 tablespoons ground cinnamon
3 ounces Everclear, or other high-proof neutral spirit
3 ounces water

Add cinnamon and Everclear to a mason jar and stir. Cover and allow to sit for two days. Strain through an extra fine filter into a clean jar and add water.

ATOMIC SWIZZLE

ALLIE STAGE, MAX'S SOUTH SEAS HIDEAWAY, GRAND RAPIDS, MI

In the tiki drink world, to "swizzle" is to mix vigorously with a swizzle stick, rapidly rubbing it between your palms. The result is a frosty, beautifully mingled drink, like this take on the Saturn made with Jamaican rum and amaro.

SERVES 1

1½ ounces Smith & Cross rum, or other Jamaican rum
¾ ounce lemon juice
½ ounce Cynar, or other amaro
½ ounce orgeat syrup
½ ounce Passion Fruit Syrup (page 10)
Mint sprig, for garnish
Lemon wheel, for garnish

GLASS: collins

Pour rum, lemon juice, amaro, and syrups into a collins glass filled with crushed ice. Swizzle until glass becomes frosty. Garnish with mint and lemon.

OTHER SPIRIT-BASED COCKTAILS: SHAKE & SIP

"No amount of physical contact could match the healing powers of a well-made cocktail."

—David Sedaris

BLOWING POINT

AURORA ANGUILLA RESORT & GOLF CLUB

Named for Anguilla's port, where lucky travelers arrive on the island, the Blowing Point cocktail is an equally welcoming blend of bourbon, passion fruit, lemon juice, and grenadine. It's so quick and easy to make that you can (virtually) shake yourself to Anguilla's beaches in a jiffy.

SERVES 1

1½ ounces Bulleit bourbon, or other bourbon whiskey
1 ounce passion fruit purée
1 ounce lemon juice
½ ounce grenadine syrup
Lemon wheel, for garnish

GLASS: rocks

Add bourbon, passion fruit purée, lemon juice, and grenadine syrup to a shaker filled with ice. Shake for a couple of seconds, and strain the mixture into a rocks glass filled with fresh ice. Garnish with a lemon wheel and passion fruit slice.

PERFECT MARGARITA

LOPESAN COSTA BÁVARO RESORT, SPA & CASINO, PUNTA CANA, DOMINICAN REPUBLIC

There's a reason they call this the Perfect Margarita. The bright citrus notes from all the fresh juices—not to mention that mango sweetness—gussy up the traditional marg, taking it to a whole new level. At the resort, they use a siphon to create a fluffy, fruity foam, but you can also blend the juices and gently pour them on top if you don't have the tool at home.

SERVES 1

2 ounces tequila, preferably a quality blanco or reposado
¾ ounce Cointreau, or other orange liqueur
1 ounce lemon juice
1 ounce mango purée (made from ripe mangoes, if available)
1 ounce pink grapefruit juice
Mint, for garnish
Slice of dehydrated grapefruit, for garnish (optional)

GLASS: chilled coupe/margarita or rocks glass

Combine the tequila, Cointreau, and freshly squeezed lemon juice in a cocktail shaker filled with ice. Shake vigorously for 15 to 20 seconds to chill and blend the ingredients thoroughly.

Create a foam by adding mango purée and grapefruit juice to a blender and blending until smooth. Strain the mixture to remove any pulp or fibers, then transfer it to a siphon. Charge the siphon with a CO_2 or N_2O cartridge according to the siphon's instructions and chill for at least 10 minutes before use. *Note: if you don't have a siphon, reserve the blended purée and gently pour on top of drink at the end.*

Strain the shaken cocktail into a chilled coupe, margarita, or rocks glass. Top the drink with the prepared mango and grapefruit foam, dispensing it gently from the siphon to create a fluffy, aromatic layer about ½-inch thick. Garnish with mint and dehydrated grapefruit, if using.

SEA AND SAND

TROY DELORT, HILTON BARBADOS RESORT

The inspiration for this tequila-based cocktail? That magical line where the sea meets the sand. Recreate the colors of the ocean with blue Curaçao and then throw a little "sand" on the rim of your glass via the salt. (Bonus points if you mix the salt with some black pepper and yellow coloring to make it more realistic.)

SERVES 1

Salt, for rimming
1½ ounces tequila
1 ounce blue Curaçao
2 ounces grapefruit juice
1 ounce Honey Syrup (page 10)
Grapefruit wedge, for garnish

GLASS: rocks

Wet the rim of the rocks glass and then dip or roll rim into the salt. Shake off excess and add a few ice cubes to the glass. Pour tequila, blue Curaçao, grapefruit juice, and honey syrup into a shaker filled with ice and give it a good shake. Strain into rimmed rocks glass and garnish with a grapefruit wedge.

FLUFFY REFRESHER

SHERVIN JOHNSON (AKA FLUFFY), MANOR BAR, ROSEWOOD BAHA MAR, THE BAHAMAS

Fluffy (or Shervin Johnson, if you must) is a bit of an icon in The Bahamas. His personality is just, well, fluffy—or at least that's how a group of travel agents described him, and their moniker stuck. Perhaps Fluffy's best-loved drink is his Refresher, a tangy and sweet blend of vodka, St-Germain, lime, and simple syrup. Add a splash of Prosecco for a little sparkle, and you'll be making Fluffy proud.

SERVES 1

2 ounces Grey Goose vodka, or other vodka
½ ounce St-Germain, or other elderflower liqueur
½ ounce lime juice
½ ounce Simple Syrup (page 10)
Splash of prosecco

GLASS: martini

Fill a shaker with ice and pour in vodka, elderflower liqueur, lime juice, and simple syrup. Give it a shake and strain into a martini glass. Top with a splash of prosecco.

THE ROAD RUNNER

JAY LITTLE, OAK HOUSE, BIRMINGHAM, AL

The reward-to-effort ratio is high on this one. You simply grab your agave spirits, Campari, and juices and shake. Then kick back with your slightly sweet, mostly sharp drink and applaud your minimal efforts.

SERVES 1

1½ ounces blanco tequila
½ ounce mezcal
¼ ounce Campari
1½ ounces pineapple juice
¼ ounce lime juice
Lime swath (peel), for garnish (optional)

GLASS: chilled martini

Pour tequila, mezcal, Campari, and juices into a shaker with ice. Give it a good shake and strain into a chilled martini glass. Garnish with lime swath, if using.

RASPBERRY TEQUILA SANGRIA

BANYAN TREE MAYAKOBA, PLAYA DEL CARMEN, MEXICO

Sangria is the perfect crowd-pleasing drink to celebrate special occasions, holidays, or simply getting the trash out in time. (Way to go, you!) This version from Banyan Tree Mayakoba takes traditional Mexican sangria and gives it a vibrant raspberry twist. While this drink is clear, you can have fun with color by putting it in rose-colored glasses. Make it the night before for the best flavor!

SERVES 6

1 (750-milliliter) bottle dry white wine
1 cup tequila
½ cup triple sec
2 tablespoons sugar
1 cup raspberries
1 sliced lime
1 sliced lemon
Soda water, to serve

GLASS: pitcher; and wine or rocks glasses

Combine white wine, tequila, triple sec, and sugar in a large pitcher. Stir until the sugar is dissolved. Add raspberries, lime, and lemon. Let the mixture sit in the refrigerator for at least 2 hours (or overnight) for the flavors to meld together. To serve, pour into a wine or rocks glass with ice and top with a splash of soda water.

JUNIPER & TONIC

ROSEWOOD BERMUDA

Inspired by the bewitching light green hue of Bermuda cedar trees (also known as junipers), this cocktail combines lime and ginger–tinged gin with melon liqueur for color and sweetness. Add egg white for a light, foamy top.

SERVES 1

2 ounces Pickering's Lime & Ginger gin, or 1½ ounces dry gin + ½ ounce Ginger Syrup (page 10)
1 ounce melon liqueur
1 ounce lime juice
½ ounce Simple Syrup (page 10)
¼ ounce egg white (from about ½ large egg)
1 ounce tonic water
Mint sprig, for garnish
Lime wedge, for garnish

GLASS: highball

Pour gin, melon liqueur, lime juice, simple syrup, and egg white into a shaker. Dry shake (without ice) for six seconds and strain into a highball glass filled with ice. Pour in tonic water and garnish with mint and lime.

RIVIERA SOUR

SEAN BIGGS, SHIPWRECKED TIKI BAR, DAVIS, CA

What do you get when you combine rich cognac, tart lemon, nutty orgeat, and tropical falernum? This fancy-schmancy cocktail—crowned with a frothy egg white to boot—that's more than fit to toast the weekend. (Or a Monday.)

SERVES 1

1½ ounces Pierre Ferrand 1840, or other cognac
½ ounce John D. Taylor's Velvet falernum, or other falernum
½ ounce orgeat syrup
1 ounce lemon juice
¾ ounce egg white (from about 1 egg)
2 dashes Saline Solution (page 11)

GLASS: chilled coupe

Pour all ingredients into a shaker. Dry shake, add ice, and shake again. Strain into a chilled coupe glass.

SOMERSET SUNSET

THE SOMERSET ON GRACE BAY, TURKS AND CAICOS

The ultimate golden hour cocktail, this sparkling stunner is a favorite in Turks and Caicos. It's easy to find out why, even if you're a few longitudinal degrees west of the islands. With just four shaken ingredients plus a tonic water topping, you can be sipping this for your own sunset in no time.

SERVES 1

2 ounces gin
1 ounce elderflower liqueur
1 ounce lemon juice
1 ounce cranberry juice
2 ounces tonic water
Mint, for garnish
Lemon wheel, for garnish

GLASS: highball

In a shaker filled with ice, add gin, elderflower liqueur, and juices. Shake well until chilled. Strain the mixture into a highball glass filled with ice and top with tonic water. Stir gently to combine and garnish with mint and lemon.

TROPICAL MARGARITA

PAWANRAT "MIND" JITTISEREESAKUL, SHIPWRECKED TIKI BAR, DAVIS, CA

There's a reason there are so many margarita variations—the tart, citrusy drink is downright delicious, and sipping one makes every day feel like summer. Shipwrecked Tiki Bar's take uses pineapple juice and passion fruit purée for some tropical zing.

SERVES 1

Simple Syrup, for rimming (page 10)
Tajín, for rimming
1½ ounces Cazcabel blanco tequila, or other blanco tequila
1½ ounces pineapple juice
¾ ounce passion fruit purée
¾ ounce agave
½ ounce lime juice
Pineapple fronds, for garnish (optional)
Passion fruit quarter, for garnish (optional)

GLASS: double old fashioned

Put simple syrup in a shallow bowl or saucer and Tajín in a separate bowl or saucer. Wet the rim of the glass with the syrup and then roll the rim of the glass in Tajín. Pour tequila, pineapple juice, passion fruit purée, agave, and lime juice into a Boston shaker with ice. Give it a good shake and pour everything into the prepared glass. Garnish with pineapple fronds and passion fruit, if using.

TA'KILL YA PAIN

ADRIFT TIKI BAR, DENVER, CO

If a classic painkiller cocktail took a vacation of its own to Mexico, this is its south of the border glow up. Swapping dark rum for tequila, Adrift Tiki Bar serves their version out of a punch bowl built for two, but feel free to use whatever vessel you've got that's large enough to handle its coconutty-agave goodness.

SERVES 2

5 ounces blanco tequila
1 ounce coconut liqueur
2 ounces orange juice
2 ounces pineapple juice
1 ounce lime juice
1 ounce coconut cream
Pineapple fronds, for garnish (optional)
Pineapple slices, for garnish (optional)
Orange slices, for garnish (optional)

GLASS: small punch bowl (24 to 36 ounces) or preferred glass

Add tequila, coconut liqueur, juices, and coconut cream to a shaker and flash blend for 5 seconds. (If you don't have a flash blender, pour all ingredients and about 12 pieces of pebble ice into a shaker and shake until ice is dissolved.) Pour drink into a small punch bowl or glass of choice filled with crushed ice, add 2 straws, and garnish with pineapple fronds, pineapple, and orange.

PINK SAND CITRUS SUNSET

RASHAD CASH, SLS BAHA MAR, THE BAHAMAS

Watermelon-based cocktails might be the loveliest of love languages. They're bright, sweet, cooling, and pink. This one is balanced with lime juice, citrus vodka, and Cointreau, which is pretty much the liquid equivalent of whispering sweet nothings.

SERVES 1

2 ounces Pink Sand Island Citrus vodka, or other citrus vodka
1 ounce Cointreau
3 ounces watermelon juice
¼ ounce lime juice
¼ ounce Simple Syrup (page 10)
Lime wheel, for garnish (optional)

GLASS: collins or preferred glass

Pour vodka, Cointreau, juices, and simple syrup into a shaker with ice. Give it a good shake and strain into a collins glass filled with fresh ice. Garnish with lime, if using.

SUNSET PARADISE

VALENTINO LONGO, DORADO BEACH, A RITZ-CARLTON RESERVE, PUERTO RICO

If drinks were only celebrated for their beauty, this one would win hands down. The three splashy layers of cranberry juice, orange-peach tequila, and butterfly pea flower–tinged vodka are as gorgeous as you can get. But that would be superficial and perpetuate unrealistic beauty standards, so luckily this drink is also pretty darn talented in the taste department.

SERVES 1

½ ounce blanco tequila
¼ ounce triple sec
1 teaspoon peach brandy
1½ ounces orange juice
¼ ounce lime juice
1½ ounces vodka
½ ounce butterfly pea flower tea
1 ounce cranberry juice
Orange slice, for garnish

GLASS: rocks

Pour tequila, triple sec, peach brandy, and juices into a shaker filled with ice and give it a good shake. In a separate small glass, mix vodka with tea. Into a rocks glass filled with ice, first pour cranberry juice, then strain tequila mixture, and top with vodka floater. Garnish with orange.

OTHER SPIRIT-BASED COCKTAILS: INFUSE AHEAD

"I drink to make other people more interesting."

—Ernest Hemingway

THE CURSE

PORCO LOUNGE & TIKI ROOM, CLEVELAND, OH

While the name of this drink might sound ominous, it's actually the tropically refreshing sort of ominous. Because passion fruit, bourbon, and ginger beer curses are way better than the ones inflicted by mummies or dead baseball players.

SERVES 1

2 ounces bourbon
2 ounces Passion Fruit Syrup (page 10)
½ ounce lime juice
2 ounces ginger beer
Cherry, for garnish
Lime wheel, for garnish (optional)

GLASS: rocks

Pour bourbon, passion fruit syrup, and lime juice into a shaker filled with ice. Give it a good shake and pour into a rocks glass with fresh ice. Top with ginger beer and garnish with cherry and lime, if using.

THE PASADENA

ANTOINE FOURNIER, BEACH HOUSE AND BAR MÉLANGÉ AT ROSEWOOD LE GUANAHANI ST. BARTH

How do you improve upon the citrusy delight that is a traditional Paloma? You add tequila **and** *mezcal, that's how. (And not just any mezcal, but a spicy, jalapeño-infused one.) That smoky kick is exactly what you need to balance the tart grapefruit and lime, without overpowering the fresh taste this drink is known for.*

SERVES 1

Spicy salt, for rimming (optional)
1 ounce blanco tequila
1 ounce Jalapeño-Infused Mezcal (below)
2½ ounces grapefruit juice
1½ ounces soda water
½ ounce agave syrup
½ ounce lime juice

GLASS: tumbler or preferred glass

Rim tumbler or preferred glass with spicy salt, if using. Fill prepared glass with ice, then pour in all ingredients. Give it a stir, add a straw, and start sipping.

Jalapeño-Infused Mezcal

MAKES ONE 750-MILLILITER BOTTLE

3 diced jalapeños, with seeds
1 (750-milliliter) bottle mezcal

Put the diced jalapeños in the mezcal and let sit at room temperature for two hours. Strain and it's ready for mixing. Best if used within a few months.

ARAKI'S MANA

TEHRAN PEFFLEY-ROUTT, MAX'S SOUTH SEAS HIDEAWAY, GRAND RAPIDS, MI

In Polynesian and Melanesian cultures, "mana" is a supernatural force that can be good or evil. I think that this mix of bold tequila, silky orgeat, and tangy citrus is definitely on the good side. For the cinnamon syrup, you can double up on the sugar for a richer mouthfeel.

SERVES 1

2 ounces tequila
½ ounce orgeat syrup
¾ ounce lime juice
¾ ounce grapefruit juice
¾ ounce Cinnamon Rich Simple Syrup (below)
1 dash Angostura bitters
Grapefruit peel cut into leaf shape, for garnish (optional)

GLASS: chilled coupe

Pour tequila, orgeat syrup, juices, cinnamon syrup, and bitters into a shaker filled with ice. Double strain into a chilled coupe glass and garnish with grapefruit peel, if using.

Cinnamon Rich Simple Syrup

MAKES 2 CUPS; 2:1 SUGAR TO WATER RATIO

2 cups sugar
1 cup water
4 cinnamon sticks

Stir the sugar into the water in a medium saucepan over high heat. Bring to a boil and stir again until the sugar fully dissolves. Reduce heat and add cinnamon sticks. Cover and simmer for about 5 minutes. Keeping the pan covered, remove from heat and let flavors meld for at least 1 hour and up to 8 hours. Strain into a mason jar or other airtight container and store in the refrigerator for up to 2 weeks.

CATAMARAN

SHANNON TEBAY, DEATH & CO, NEW YORK, NY

Don the Beachcomber is a bit of a legend in the tiki world. He shared Caribbean and South Pacific flavors with mainland America back in the 1930s, creating cocktails like the Zombie using Don's Mix. Whip up a batch of his eponymous cinnamon grapefruit syrup to recreate Death & Co's gin-based Catamaran.

SERVES 1

1½ ounces Bimini gin, or other dry gin or light rum
½ ounce Perry's Tot navy strength gin, or other navy strength gin
½ ounce Aperol, or other bitter orange liqueur
1 ounce Don's Mix (opposite)
½ ounce lemon juice
½ ounce Coco Lopez, or other coconut cream
Edible orchid, for garnish (optional)
Cinnamon stick, for garnish (optional)

GLASS: tulip or preferred glass

Pour gins, Aperol, Don's Mix, lemon juice, and coconut cream into a shaker filled with 12 or so pieces of pebble ice. Whip shake, or shake until ice is dissolved, and dump into a tulip glass or glass of choice filled with crushed ice. Garnish with an orchid and a cinnamon stick, if using.

Don's Mix

MAKES 3½ CUPS

1 cup granulated sugar
1 cup water
3 cinnamon sticks
2 cups grapefruit juice (about 3 or 4 grapefruits)

Combine the sugar, water, and cinnamon sticks in a medium saucepan over high heat. Bring to a boil, then simmer for 10 minutes. Remove from the heat and let sit for another 10 minutes. Strain into a heatproof jar, discarding the cinnamon sticks, and cool completely. Add the grapefruit juice to the syrup and mix to combine. Cover and keep refrigerated for up to 2 weeks.

LA COPA BANYAN MARGARITA

BANYAN TREE MAYAKOBA, PLAYA DEL CARMEN, MEXICO

Proving you can never have too many margaritas (just maybe not all at the same time), this riff combines black pepper–infused mezcal with the classic lime and agave flavors. The result is a tart, spicy, and smoky sip that could rise to the top of your favorite marg list. The mezcal takes a day or two to infuse, so plan ahead.

SERVES 1

Salt, for rimming
1½ ounces young mezcal
½ ounce Black Pepper–Infused Mezcal (below)
1 ounce lime juice
½ ounce agave
Orange wedge, for garnish

GLASS: old fashioned

Rim an old-fashioned glass with salt and fill with ice. Pour mezcals, lime juice, and agave into a shaker and shake vigorously for 10 seconds. Strain into prepared glass and add orange wedge garnish.

Black Pepper–Infused Mezcal

MAKES ONE 750-MILLILITER BOTTLE

1 (750-milliliter) bottle mezcal
2 tablespoons cracked black peppercorns

Add the peppercorns to the mezcal and stir. Let it sit for 24 to 48 hours at room temperature, then strain mixture with a fine sieve or coffee filter into a clean bottle.

BUBBLY BREEZE

PINE CAY, TURKS AND CAICOS

While other drinks might get watered down if you take too long to drink them, this sweet, bubbly cocktail only gets better. The large grapefruit ice sphere slowly melts, infusing its bright citrus flavor into this downright darling of a cocktail.

SERVES 1

1½ ounces Bombay Sapphire gin, or other gin
½ ounce elderflower syrup
Splash of Angostura bitters
Grapefruit ice sphere (ruby red grapefruit juice and a couple drops of aromatic bitters frozen into a large sphere mold)
3 ounces champagne
Rosemary sprig, for garnish
Lemon peel, for garnish (optional)

GLASS: champagne coupe or preferred glass

In a mixing glass filled with ice, add gin, elderflower syrup, and bitters. Shake well and strain into a champagne coupe glass. Add grapefruit ice sphere to the glass and fill with champagne. Garnish with rosemary and lemon peel, if using.

SHE'S THE EMPRESS, NOT THE CONCUBINE

GRACE TOMCZAK, MAKFAM, DENVER, CO

You know how you're always slurping up every last drop of pineapple curry at your favorite Thai spot? This is like that in yummy cocktail form. If you haven't yet experimented with baijiu (clear Chinese grain spirits), this is the perfect start.

SERVES 1

1½ ounces pisco
¾ ounce baijiu
1½ ounces pineapple juice
¾ ounce Thai Bird Curry Syrup (opposite)
½ ounce lime juice
¼ ounce coconut vinegar
Mint sprig, for garnish
Pineapple candy or pineapple fronds, for garnish (optional)

GLASS: tiki mug

Pour pisco, baijiu, pineapple juice, Thai bird curry syrup, lime juice, and coconut vinegar into a shaker filled with ice. Give it a good shake and dirty dump (pour with ice) into a tiki mug. Garnish with mint and pineapple, if using.

Thai Bird Curry Syrup

MAKES ABOUT 3 CUPS

1 cup sugar
2 tablespoons crushed red pepper flakes
⅓ cup Madras curry powder
2½ cups water

Stir the sugar, red pepper flakes, and curry powder into the water in a medium saucepan over high heat. Bring to a boil and stir again until the sugar fully dissolves. Remove pan from heat and let cool before straining into a mason jar or other airtight container. Store in the refrigerator for up to 2 weeks.

THE LITTLE TIGER

GRACE TOMCZAK, MAKFAM, DENVER, CO

Szechuan peppercorns are known for their tongue-tingling effects, and while your taste buds aren't going to go fully MIA on you here, you'll get a whisper of their buzz from the infused tequila. Combined with the fresh mandarin, it's a really fresh, tingly sip.

SERVES 1

1½ ounces Szechuan Peppercorn and Five Spice–Infused Tequila (below)
½ ounce vermouth bianco
1 ounce Mandarin Vanilla Syrup (opposite)
½ ounce lemon juice
¼ ounce Coconut Syrup (page 10)
Mint sprigs for garnish

GLASS: tiki mug

Pour tequila, vermouth, mandarin vanilla syrup, lemon juice, and coconut syrup into a shaker filled with ice. Give it a good shake and dirty dump (pour with ice) into tiki mug. Garnish with mint.

Szechuan Peppercorn and Five Spice–Infused Tequila

MAKES ONE 750-MILLILITER BOTTLE

1 (750-milliliter) bottle reposado tequila
1½ tablespoons ground Szechuan peppercorns
1½ tablespoons five-spice powder

Combine tequila with peppercorns and five-spice powder. Give it a stir and allow it to sit overnight. Strain into a clean bottle.

Mandarin Vanilla Syrup

MAKES 1½ CUPS

1 cup sugar
1 cup mandarin juice, strained
¼ teaspoon vanilla extract

Stir sugar and vanilla into mandarin juice until all sugar is dissolved. Store in a mason jar or other airtight container in the refrigerator for up to 2 weeks.

PYT

GRACE TOMCZAK, MAKFAM, DENVER, CO

This drink isn't just pretty to look at, it's also hugely gulpable. With its silky mouthfeel and tropically herbaceous flavors from the coconut and aperitifs, it's a balanced blend of loveliness.

SERVES 1

1½ ounces reposado tequila
¼ ounce Suze, or other clear aperitif
¼ ounce Lillet Rosé, or other aperitif, preferably pink
¾ ounce lemon juice
½ ounce Hibiscus Vanilla Syrup (below)
½ ounce Coconut Syrup (page 10)
Dehydrated or fresh lemon wheel, for garnish

GLASS: collins or preferred glass

Pour tequila, aperitifs, lemon juice, and syrups into a shaker filled with ice. Shake for 10 to 15 seconds and strain into a collins glass or glass of choice filled with fresh ice. Garnish with lemon.

Hibiscus Vanilla Syrup

MAKES ABOUT 1½ CUPS

1 cup sugar
1 cup water
¼ cup dried hibiscus
⅛ teaspoon vanilla extract

Stir the sugar, hibiscus, and vanilla into the water in a medium saucepan over high heat. Bring to a boil and stir again until the sugar fully dissolves. Remove pan from heat and let cool before straining into a mason jar or other airtight container. Store in the refrigerator for up to 2 weeks.

SOMETHIN' TEQUILA

PORCO LOUNGE & TIKI ROOM, CLEVELAND, OH

A cross between a margarita (hello, tequila and lime juice) and a rum barrel (yo, ho, ho, tropical juices) this cocktail is fruity, sour, and recommended by agave lovers everywhere. Pucker up.

SERVES 1

3 ounces reposado tequila
1 ounce lime juice
1 ounce pineapple juice
1 ounce orange juice
1 ounce Simple Syrup (page 10)
½ ounce Passion Fruit Syrup (page 10)
Pineapple fronds, for garnish
Cherry, for garnish
Lime wheel, for garnish (optional)

GLASS: hurricane

Pour tequila, juices, and syrups into a shaker filled with ice. Give it a good shake and strain into a hurricane glass filled with fresh ice. Garnish with pineapple fronds, a cherry, and a lime wheel, if using.

FROZEN LIBATIONS

"Time flies when you're having rum."

—Erik Voskamp

PIÑA CON LOCA

HENRY OTTRIX, XIQUITA RESTAURANTE Y BAR, DENVER, CO

Jazz up your piña colada game with pimento dram, a Jamaican allspice liqueur that acts as a spiced sweetener. Swapping the typical rum for vodka and brandy in this recipe allows the pineapple and coconut to really pop.

SERVES 1

1 ounce vodka
½ ounce brandy
½ ounce pimento dram, or allspice liqueur
1 ounce pineapple juice
¾ ounce coconut cream
½ ounce lime juice
Lime wedge, for garnish
Cherry, for garnish

GLASS: collins

Pour vodka, brandy, pimento dram, pineapple juice, coconut cream, and lime juice into a blender. Add a scoop of ice and blend until smooth. Pour into a collins glass and garnish with lime and cherry.

FROZEN CHI CHI

ADRIFT TIKI BAR, DENVER, CO

In this take on a frozen piña colada, the acidulated pineapple juice (or lime juice) keeps it on the right side of sappy-sweet territory. Because no one wants to be on the wrong side of sappy-sweet.

SERVES 1

2 ounces vodka
½ ounce maraschino liqueur
2 ounces pineapple juice
1½ ounces coconut cream
½ ounce Acid-Adjusted Pineapple Juice (page 51), or lime juice
6 chunks of frozen pineapple
5 drops Saline Solution (page 11), or pinch of salt
Pineapple fronds, for garnish
Edible orchid, for garnish

GLASS: tall pilsner or preferred glass

Add vodka, maraschino liqueur, pineapple juice, coconut cream, acid-adjusted pineapple juice, frozen pineapple, and saline to a blender. Add one cup of crushed ice and blend until smooth. Pour into a tall pilsner glass or glass of choice, add a straw, and garnish with pineapple fronds and orchid.

FROZEN HOUND

CHRIS MOSES, SURF HOUND, BIRMINGHAM, AL

The beach is a happy place, made happier with a frosty beverage in hand (or nestled into the sand). This easy blend of spiced rums, pineapple and orange juices, and coconut cream or syrup is like a fruity, icy passport to the beach, even when you're landlocked.

SERVES 1

1 ounce spiced rum
1 ounce Kraken spiced rum, or other high-proof spiced rum
1½ ounces pineapple juice
1 ounce orange juice
1 ounce coconut cream, or Coconut Syrup (page 10)
Nutmeg, for garnish

GLASS: collins

Pour rums, juices, and coconut cream into a blender. Add a scoop of ice and blend until smooth. Pour into a collins glass and garnish with nutmeg.

ESPRESSO MARTINI

ANGEL HORTA LUPIAC, KIMPTON SURFCOMBER HOTEL, MIAMI, FL

If you're already obsessed with espresso martinis, you're going to be over the moon for this frozen version. Bonus: it'll perk you up for your night's (or day's; this drink is just as good when the sun's up) adventures.

SERVES 1

1 ounce premium vodka
½ ounce Baileys chocolate liqueur, or other chocolate liqueur
4 ounces cappuccino mix
1 ounce cold brew coffee
Strawberry slice, for garnish

GLASS: martini

Into a blender filled with a couple ice cubes, pour vodka, chocolate liqueur, cappuccino mix, and cold brew coffee. Blend until smooth. Pour into chilled martini glass and garnish with slice of strawberry.

SOUTHSIDE

PLAYA GRANDE BEACH CLUB, DOMINICAN REPUBLIC

Mint has loads of health properties, so drinking this frozen Southside is kind of like drinking gin-spiked green juice, right? At the Playa Grande Beach Club, they serve a virgin version when guests arrive, so this refresher is just as good without the booze.

SERVES 1

2 ounces Hendrick's gin, or other gin
2 ounces lime juice
2 ounces Simple Syrup (page 10)
15 to 20 mint leaves, plus extra for garnish

GLASS: rocks or anything fun

Pour a large scoop of ice, gin, lime juice, simple syrup, and mint leaves into a blender. Blend until smooth, then pour into a rocks glass and garnish with mint leaves.

POOLSIDE DRAGON FRUIT MARGARITA

KEEGAN LABRADOR, MISTER OSO, DENVER, CO

For this brightest of bright pink drinks, you blend dragon fruit simple syrup with lime, tequila, and sotol (a grassy Mexican spirit). Besides the vibrant hue, the dragon fruit gives it a soft sweetness, but you can just as easily swap prickly pear or strawberries for the syrup.

SERVES 1

1 ounce blanco tequila
½ ounce sotol
⅛ ounce Three Spirit Livener (optional)
⅛ ounce John D. Taylor's Velvet falernum
3 ounces Dragon Fruit Simple Syrup (opposite)
½ lime, cut into quarters
Mint sprig, for garnish

GLASS: margarita or preferred glass

Pour tequila, sotol, Three Spirit Livener (if using), falernum, dragon fruit simple syrup, and lime into a blender. Blend on medium speed until the lime is broken down as much as possible. If necessary, strain through a mesh strainer to remove large pieces and add back to blender. Add 2 cups of crushed ice and blend on low/medium speed until ice is dissolved. Pour into a margarita glass or glass of choice and garnish with mint, if using.

Dragon Fruit Simple Syrup

MAKES ABOUT ⅔ CUP

3½ ounces (100 grams) dragon fruit purée
¼ cup water
¼ cup granulated sugar

In a blender, combine dragon fruit purée with water and sugar. Blend until sugar is completely dissolved. Store in a mason jar or other airtight container in the refrigerator for up to 30 days.

ISLAND BLISS

OIL NUT BAY, BRITISH VIRGIN ISLANDS

For this frosty refresher, you can go either high octane with the rum, or no octane without it. It's going to be great either way. Mango juice forms the foundation of this creamy, cooling drink that definitely lives up to its name.

SERVES 1

1½ ounces Bacardí Limón rum, or other citrus rum (optional)
1 ounce mango juice
¾ ounce lime juice
¾ ounce coconut cream
8 to 10 mint leaves

GLASS: rocks or collins

Pour a scoop of crushed ice, rum (if using), juices, coconut cream, and mint leaves into a blender. Blend until smooth. Pour into your glass of choice.

ORANGE CREAMSICLE

LURE, ATLANTA, GA

The orange creamsicle frozen treat was created by an 11-year-old in 1905, but this modern version is entirely for grown-ups. The blend of orange spirits and juice with lime, saline, and a creamy coconut mix is like a boozy remix of childhood.

SERVES 1

1 ounce orange vodka
½ ounce orange liqueur
½ ounce Licor 43
1¼ ounces orange juice
1 ounce Coconut Mix (below)
¼ ounce lime juice
½ teaspoon liquid shio koji, or coconut aminos
2 drops Saline Solution (page 11)
1 drop vanilla extract
1 drop yellow + ½ drop red organic food coloring (optional)
Orange slice, for garnish

GLASS: rocks

Pour orange vodka, orange liqueur, Licor 43, orange juice, coconut mix, lime juice, shio koji, saline solution, vanilla, and food coloring (if using) into a blender. Add an ounce of ice cubes and blend until smooth. Pour into glass and garnish with orange.

Coconut Mix

MAKES 2½ CUPS

1 (15-ounce) can Coco Lopez, or other cream of coconut
5 ounces coconut milk

Using a stick blender or whisk, mix the cream of coconut and coconut milk together until smooth. Store in a mason jar or other airtight container in the refrigerator for up to 1 week.

MOCKTAILS

"Let's raise a toast to the coast."

–Unknown

MATCHA COLADA SPRITZ

ADRIANO VENTURINI, EDEN ROC CAP CANA, DOMINICAN REPUBLIC

Like a classic piña colada but made lighter and more refreshing with vibrant matcha, this spritzy take is a deliciously bubbly east-meets-west love story. It's tropical, it's bright, it's highly sippable—and, oh yeah, it couldn't be quicker (or easier) to make.

SERVES 1

2 ounces pineapple juice
1 ounce coconut cream
½ ounce Simple Syrup (page 10)
1 bar spoon of matcha
Soda water
Pineapple leaf, for garnish (optional)

GLASS: champagne flute or preferred glass

Fill the champagne flute with pineapple juice, coconut cream, simple syrup, and matcha. Give it a stir to mix, then fill the rest of the glass with soda water. Garnish with pineapple leaf, if using.

BABY BEACH

HYATT REGENCY ARUBA RESORT, SPA & CASINO, PALM BEACH, ARUBA

Inspired by Aruba's white beaches and turquoise sea, this stunner is made from just three ingredients. You get sweetness from the coconut cream, a spunky bite from the ginger beer, and then the blue grenadine gives it that dreamy, oceany hue. Obviously best sipped on an Aruban beach, but your couch makes for a close second.

SERVES 1

1 ounce coconut cream, divided
4 ounces Fever-Tree ginger beer, or other ginger beer, divided
1 dash blue grenadine
Lemon wheel, for garnish
Mint, for garnish
Raspberries, for garnish

GLASS: tumbler

Fill a tumbler with ice. Pour in half of the coconut cream and ginger beer, and all of the blue grenadine. Give it a stir. Place lemon wheel on the drink and then pour the other half of the coconut cream and ginger beer. Garnish with mint leaves and raspberries.

JUNGLE JUICE

ANGEL HORTA LUPIAC,
KIMPTON SURFCOMBER HOTEL, MIAMI, FL

This is not the jungle juice you drank out of trash cans in college. This is a super sophisticated, super refreshing drink that mingles the tartness of lime with the coolness of cucumber. You could make just one, but you may want to batch it up—it's that good.

SERVES 1

1 ounce Simple Syrup (page 10)
1 ounce lime juice
½ ounce cucumber juice
Lemon lime soda
Cucumber slice, for garnish

GLASS: collins

Fill a shaker with ice and pour in simple syrup and juices. Give it a good shake and then strain into a collins glass filled with ice. Pour lemon lime soda to the top of the glass and garnish with a slice of cucumber.

COOL PASSION
ROSEWOOD BERMUDA

The tropical bite of the Rosewood Bermuda's Cool Passion pairs perfectly with a sunny beach day, but let's be real: we're happy to have one in hand during a rain- or snowstorm, too. Pour it all into your favorite beer goblet and toast the sun/rain/snow.

SERVES 1

1 ounce mango purée
½ ounce lime juice
½ ounce Honey Syrup (page 10)
4 ounces ginger beer
Cucumber slices, for garnish
Mint, for garnish
Lime wedge, for garnish

GLASS: beer goblet or preferred glass

Fill a shaker with ice and pour in mango purée, lime juice, and honey syrup. Give it a good shake, strain into a beer goblet or glass of choice, top with ginger beer, and garnish with cucumber, mint, and lime.

AMANYARA COOLER

AMANYARA, TURKS AND CAICOS

Kind of a choose-your-own-adventure sort of mocktail, the Amanyara Cooler is a versatile sip. Want something sweeter? Add simple syrup. Looking for something boozy? Throw in a shot of tequila. However you make it, you'll be glad you did.

SERVES 1

1½ ounces grapefruit juice
½ ounce lime juice
½ ounce Simple Syrup (page 10, optional)
8 mint leaves, plus more for garnish
Club soda
Grapefruit wedge, for garnish

GLASS: highball

Combine juices, simple syrup (if using), and mint in a blender. Blend on high speed for 20 seconds, until smooth. Fill a highball glass with ice and finely strain blended drink into the glass. Top with club soda and gently stir to combine. Garnish with mint and grapefruit.

P.O.G.

ADRIFT TIKI BAR, DENVER, CO

Hawaii is linked with a whole lot of tropical drinks, but P.O.G. should definitely be shortlisted for MGHB (Most Glorious Hawaiian Beverage). It stands for passion fruit, orange, and guava for the uninitiated, and one sip will transport you to Maui for those imaginary MGHB awards.

SERVES 1

2 ounces orange juice
1 ounce Passion Fruit Syrup (page 10), or
 2 ounces passion fruit juice or nectar
1 ounce Guava Syrup (page 10), or 2 ounces guava juice or nectar
4 ounces water
Orange slice, for garnish
Edible orchid or pineapple frond, for garnish

GLASS: bamboo mug or preferred glass

Add orange juice, passion fruit syrup, guava syrup, and water to a shaker and flash blend for 5 seconds. (If you don't have a flash blender, pour all ingredients and about 12 pieces of pebble ice into a shaker and shake until ice is dissolved.) Pour drink into a bamboo mug filled with crushed ice and garnish with orange and orchid.

PEACH MOCKTAIL MULE

OMNI SAN DIEGO, CA

Melding the flavors of sun-ripened peaches with the spicy punch of a good ginger beer, this non-alcoholic spin on the mule might become your new favorite. Use fresh peaches if they're in season, but canned or defrosted frozen work in a pinch for your winter cravings.

SERVES 1

3 peach slices
¾ ounce lime juice
½ ounce agave
3 dashes non-alcoholic peach bitters
Owen's ginger beer, or other ginger beer
Lime wheels or slices, for garnish
Peach slices (optional)

GLASS: copper mule mug

Place peaches in a shaker and muddle to release juices. Add ice, lime juice, agave, and peach bitters and give it a shake. Strain into mule mug with ice and top with ginger beer. Garnish with lime and peach slices, if using.

CITRUS MARGARITA

ARMANDO DZIB, CHABLÉ MAROMA, RIVIERA MAYA, MEXICO

A mix of macerated cardamom pods and four different juices, this drink is an entire stratum of tangy, citrusy flavors. Make it even more margarita-esque by rimming your glass with black sesame and chili salt, just as they do on the Riviera Maya beaches.

SERVES 1

10 cardamom pods
½ ounce Simple Syrup (page 10)
1½ ounces grapefruit juice
1½ ounces pineapple juice
1 ounce lime juice
1 ounce mandarin juice
Chili salt, for rimming
Black sesame, for rimming
Dried grapefruit, for garnish
Pineapple stalks, for garnish (optional)

GLASS: rocks

In a shaker, add the cardamom pods and simple syrup so they soften. Allow to sit for about 10 minutes. Add juices and give it a good shake. Mix the chili salt and black sesame together in a shallow bowl or saucer. Wet the rim of the rocks glass, dip or roll in the sesame-salt mix, and add a large ice cube. Triple strain the drink into the glass and garnish with dried grapefruit and pineapple stalks, if using.

PASSION BY

MONKEYBAR, TOWN AND COUNTRY RESORT, SAN DIEGO, CA

This recipe that combines pineapple, lemon, an agave non-alcoholic spirit, and more tropical fruit shows why mocktails can be just as sophisticated as traditional cocktails. If you can't find the Corazon purée, feel free to swap an equal amount of any of its fruit purées.

SERVES 1

1½ ounces Seedlip Notas de Agave non-alcoholic spirit, or other n/a tequila
½ ounce Honey Syrup (page 10)
½ ounce The Perfect Purée of Napa Valley El Corazon purée, or a mix of passion fruit, blood orange, and/or pomegranate purée
½ ounce pineapple juice
¼ ounce lemon juice
Sparkling water
Slice of blood orange, for garnish

GLASS: collins

Pour non-alcoholic spirit, honey syrup, fruit purée, and juices into a shaker filled with ice. Give it a good shake and strain into a collins glass filled with fresh ice. Top with sparkling water and garnish with blood orange.

BEACHY SNACKS

"Eat like you're
on vacation every day."
—Unknown

BEST EVER GUACAMOLE

Jazz up your mashed avocado game with fresh cilantro and a sprinkling of cotija cheese. The jalapeño here is optional, but definitely don't skip the onion (for crunch) and fresh lime (for brightening). Easily scaled up for parties or down for solo nights. Serve with tortilla chips or pile it on tacos, burritos, or burgers.

SERVES 4 TO 6

2 ripe avocados, pit and rind removed
1 Roma tomato, diced
¼ cup finely diced yellow onion
1 garlic clove, minced
½ jalapeño, seeds removed and finely diced (optional)
2 tablespoons chopped cilantro
1 to 2 tablespoons lime juice
Salt, to taste
Sprinkling of cotija cheese

In a medium bowl, combine the avocados, tomato, onion, garlic, jalapeño (if using), cilantro, lime juice, and salt. Mash it all together until it's well combined, but still slightly chunky. Sprinkle with the cotija cheese and serve.

SPICY BAKED PLANTAIN CHIPS

Warning: You'll be devouring these crispy, kicky chips by the handful. The high starch content in unripe plantains stands up better to baking, so reach for the green ones for these healthy chips.

SERVES 4

2 unripe plantains
2 tablespoons olive or avocado oil
1 teaspoon chipotle powder
½ teaspoon cumin
½ teaspoon salt
Zest of 1 lime

Preheat the oven to 375°F and line a baking sheet with parchment paper.

Peel the plantains. (Use a knife for the green, unripe ones with hard-to-remove peels.) Slice very thinly into uniform slices, using a mandolin if you have one. Otherwise try to slice them as thinly as you can—too thick and they won't crisp up in the oven.

Toss the plantain slices with oil, chipotle powder, cumin, and salt in a large bowl. Spread the slices in a single layer on the prepared baking sheet. Bake for 15 to 20 minutes, turning halfway through the cooking time. When they're getting golden around the edges, they are ready. Remove from oven and sprinkle with the lime zest.

Eat immediately, or store for a day or two in an airtight container.

AREA 31 HUMMUS

AREA 31, KIMPTON EPIC HOTEL, MIAMI, FL

How does Miami do hummus? They load it up with olive oil and top it with grilled pineapple, red bell pepper, and creamy avocado. Serve with toasted pita or more veggies and take a dip.

SERVES 6

HUMMUS

1 (15-ounce) can garbanzo beans, drained
½ cup boiling water from beans (see instructions)
1 cup olive oil
⅓ cup tahini
1 clove garlic, grated
1½ teaspoons cumin
1 teaspoon paprika
½ teaspoon ground coriander
¼ to ⅓ cup lemon juice (about 1 lemon)
½ teaspoon ascorbic acid (optional)
Salt, to taste

TROPICAL TOPPING

½ cup small diced grilled red bell pepper
½ cup small diced avocado
½ cup small diced grilled pineapple
½ cup small diced grilled red onion
½ cup chopped cilantro
¼ cup lime juice
¼ cup sherry vinegar
½ cup olive oil

For the hummus: In a pot over medium-high heat, boil the drained garbanzo beans with 1 cup of water for 15 to 20 minutes, or until tender. Reserve ½ cup of the liquid. Put the boiled garbanzo beans and ½ cup of liquid, olive oil, tahini, garlic, cumin, paprika, coriander, lemon juice, ascorbic acid (if using), and salt in a food processor. Mix until smooth.

For the tropical topping: Place the bell pepper, avocado, pineapple, red onion, cilantro, lime juice, sherry vinegar, and olive oil in a large bowl. Toss to coat. Set aside and serve with hummus when ready.

SPAM MUSUBI

Spam musubi—a kind of Hawaiian-Japanese onigiri fusion—has been a beloved food in Hawaii for nearly a century, and now the rest of the world is catching up. Spam sales keep on climbing, and besides its versatility and affordability, that growth could be because more and more people are making this quintessential Hawaiian snack at home.

MAKES 8 TO 10 PIECES

2 cups sushi rice
1 tablespoon rice vinegar
1 (12-ounce) container Spam
½ cup sugar
¼ cup oyster sauce
¼ cup soy sauce
3 to 4 sheets sushi nori
2 tablespoons vegetable oil
Furikake

Soak, rinse, and cook the sushi rice according to package directions. Once prepared, stir in the rice vinegar.

Slice the Spam into 8 to 10 lengthwise slices, depending on your desired thickness. In a small bowl, mix the sugar, oyster sauce, and soy sauce. Place the Spam and sauce in a large ziplock bag and marinate for about 10 minutes.

Cut each nori sheet into thirds and set aside.

Heat oil in a skillet over medium-high heat. Cook the Spam until just starting to brown, about 2 to 3 minutes on each side.

Take about ⅓ cup rice and form it tightly into a rectangle, mimicking the size and shape of the Spam. The best way to do this is with a rice mold, but if you don't have one just pack the rice as tightly as possible. (You can even use the Spam container as a cheat.) Place the rice rectangle across the strip of nori and sprinkle with furikake. Place the Spam on top of rice and wrap it up. Use a little water to help the nori edges seal.

CRAB BRIOCHE

IBIZA GRAN HOTEL, SPAIN

They know a thing or two about decadence in Ibiza, like loading sweet, sweet crab meat onto sweet, sweet brioche. This recipe makes a full loaf of crab brioche, but you can scale it down if you're not feeding a crustacean-loving crowd.

SERVES 6

1 loaf brioche bread
¼ cup butter
1 pound cooked crab meat
Tartar Sauce (below)
Sliced pickles
Fresh sprouts

Cut the brioche loaf down the top without completely slicing it through, like a butterfly. Add a little butter and toast on a grill over medium heat until golden. Place crab inside, then top with tartar sauce, sliced pickles, and fresh sprouts.

Tartar Sauce

MAKES ABOUT 2 CUPS

1 cup mayonnaise
¼ cup sliced pickles
¼ cup capers
¼ cup chopped scallions
½ cup chopped parsley

Put the mayonnaise, pickles, capers, and scallions in a blender and blend for 30 seconds. Stir in the chopped parsley. Allow the flavors to meld for at least 30 minutes. Store in an airtight container in the refrigerator for up to 1 week.

JERK-SPICED CHICKEN WINGS

MONKEYBAR, TOWN AND COUNTRY RESORT, SAN DIEGO, CA

You'll definitely be licking your fingers after eating these Monkeybar wings. The mix of sweet chili sauce with spicy jerk seasoning packs a powerful flavor punch. Cook the wings however you prefer—baked, fried, or grilled—and then the sauce comes together in a flash.

MAKES 10 WINGS

10 chicken wings
3 tablespoons jerk seasoning
⅔ cup Thai sweet chili sauce
⅓ cup hoisin
¼ cup cilantro, chopped, for garnish
2 tablespoons white and/or black sesame seeds, for garnish

Cook wings to 165°F internal temperature. You can bake them in the oven for 40 to 45 minutes (flipping halfway) at 400°F; fry in batches for 8 to 10 minutes in 375°F oil; or grill over medium-high heat for 20 to 25 minutes (turning every so often).

In a dry skillet over medium-low heat, lightly toast the jerk seasoning, moving the spices around frequently for a couple minutes, until fragrant. Combine the toasted seasoning with Thai sweet chili sauce and hoisin in a mixing bowl. Stir until fully incorporated.

When wings are almost done, transfer the sauce to a small pot and heat over medium-low heat, until hot. Put the cooked wings in a large bowl and cover with the heated sauce. Toss it all together to fully coat the wings. Garnish with fresh cilantro and sesame seeds.

PULLED PORK SLIDERS

Ideally, you'd cook an entire pig in a hand-dug, underground pit. But if you don't have a pit or any rogue hogs in your backyard, a slow cooker and store-bought pork butt or shoulder works almost as well. Load all that pull-apart-tender pork on—what else?—toasted Hawaiian rolls.

SERVES 4 TO 6

2 to 2½ pounds pork butt or shoulder, excess fat trimmed
¾ teaspoon salt
½ teaspoon black pepper
½ cup pineapple juice
1 teaspoon rice wine vinegar
1 teaspoon soy sauce
1 clove garlic, minced
1 (½-inch) knob ginger, grated
⅛ teaspoon cayenne (optional)
6 Hawaiian rolls
Barbecue sauce (optional)

SPECIAL EQUIPMENT: slow cooker

Place the pork in a slow cooker and coat with salt and pepper. Pour in the pineapple juice, rice wine vinegar, soy sauce, garlic, ginger, and cayenne, if using. Cover and cook on low for 6 to 8 hours, until the pork is pull-apart tender. Shred with two forks.

Toast Hawaiian rolls and load up with the pulled pork. Add a spoonful of barbecue sauce to each slider, if desired.

FROZEN FRUIT SHAVE ICE

Recreate Hawaiian shave ice at home armed only with a microplane and frozen fruit (and maybe gloves so your hands don't go totally numb while grating). I like to use a blend of frozen peaches, strawberries, and mango, with a wild card frozen cucumber thrown in to cut the sweetness. I top my icy tower with sweetened condensed milk and Tajín, but really you can use whatever you have on hand that sounds good.

SERVES 1

½ cup frozen peaches
½ cup frozen strawberries
½ cup frozen mango
½ cucumber, frozen
Sweetened condensed milk or honey, for drizzling
Tajín, for sprinkling

SPECIAL EQUIPMENT: microplane

Chill a serving bowl in the freezer for at least 15 minutes. Grate the fruit and cucumber directly into the chilled bowl. Fluff it around a bit as you go so you get each flavor in every bite.

Drizzle sweetened condensed milk or honey over the top of the fruit bowl and sprinkle with Tajín. Eat immediately!

BLACKENED FISH TACOS

JW MARRIOTT MARCO ISLAND, FL

These fish tacos take Cajun-spiced mahi-mahi and load it up with creamy chipotle lime aioli, crumbly queso fresco, and crunchy cabbage slaw. Perfect for Taco Tuesday, or any day of the week.

MAKES 3 TACOS

FISH

6 ounces mahi-mahi (2 ounces per taco)
1 cup canola oil
¼ cup lemon juice (about 1 lemon)
1½ tablespoons Cajun spice
1½ tablespoons garlic powder
1½ tablespoons fresh thyme
1 tablespoon paprika
Salt and pepper, to taste

CHIPOTLE LIME AIOLI

1 chipotle pepper in adobo sauce
1 lime, zested and juiced
1 garlic clove, minced
2 cups mayonnaise

TACOS

6 corn tortillas
3 ounces cabbage slaw
Queso fresco
1 radish, thinly sliced
2 tablespoons cilantro, chopped

To marinate the fish, combine the oil, lemon juice, Cajun spice, garlic powder, thyme, paprika, salt, and pepper in a bowl. Mix well and pour over the fish. Marinate in the refrigerator for 20 minutes.

Make the chipotle lime aioli by placing the chipotle pepper, lime zest and juice, and garlic in a blender. Blend until smooth. Pour the mixture into a bowl and add the mayonnaise. Stir until fully combined.

To cook the fish, place a tablespoon of oil in a skillet over medium heat. Sear the fish for about 3 minutes per side, depending on thickness. When fully cooked, remove from the heat and set aside.

Assemble the tacos by stacking 2 corn tortillas and filling each with 1 ounce cabbage slaw, 1 piece cooked mahi, a drizzle of chipotle lime aioli, a sprinkle of queso fresco, a few radish slices, and cilantro.

TROPICAL SMOOTHIE BOWL

Every good beach day starts with fresh fruit, and the banana, dragon fruit, and Greek yogurt in this smoothie bowl is perfect to power you through a rousing beach volleyball game (or, more likely, lounging in the sand for eight hours). Coconut flakes and sliced kiwi make for a striking topping against the bright pink bowl.

SERVES 1

1 cup plain Greek yogurt
3 ½ ounces (100 grams) dragon fruit frozen purée
1 ripe banana
1 kiwi, sliced
Coconut flakes

Place the yogurt, dragon fruit purée, and banana in a blender. Blend until smooth. Pour into a bowl and top with sliced kiwi and coconut flakes.

SHRIMP KABOBS AL PASTOR

SANTIAGO GOMEZ, PALO SANTO, ATLANTA, GA

Everyone knows that eating food on a stick is just more fun. This recipe skewers—literally—traditional Mexican pastor, taking its sweet pineapple mingled with guajillo chiles to coat grilled skewered shrimp. You can eat these little crustaceans on their own or make tacos out of them (I recommend corn tortillas and red onion). Whichever way you choose, be sure to slather on as much of that rich pineapple brown butter sauce as humanly possible.

MAKES 5 KABOBS

SHRIMP

¾ cup canola oil
1 tablespoon achiote paste
2 to 3 guajillo chiles, seeded and soaked in hot water for 10 minutes
1 garlic clove
½ teaspoon salt
1 pound medium shrimp, peeled and deveined

PINEAPPLE BROWN BUTTER SAUCE

1 pineapple, stem, base, and skin removed and cut into chunks
1 cup (2 sticks) unsalted butter

Make the marinade for the shrimp by combining the oil, achiote paste, guajillo chiles, garlic, and salt in a blender. Blend until it makes a paste. Put the paste and shrimp in a large bowl and coat the shrimp with the paste. Cover and refrigerate for 30 minutes.

To make the pineapple brown butter sauce, place the pineapple in a blender and blend into a juice. Strain the pineapple juice into a small pot (discarding solids) and cook over low heat for 10 minutes. In a separate pot, melt the butter over medium heat. Once the butter is amber and has a rich, nutty fragrance, remove from the heat. Slowly strain the brown butter into the pineapple juice. Use a hand blender (or pour into traditional blender) to blend until smooth.

Preheat the grill. Divide the marinated shrimp into fifths. Skewer onto five metal skewers and refrigerate for 20 more minutes.

Place the kabobs on the grill and cook for 3 to 4 minutes on each side. Serve with pineapple sauce. You can brush the sauce on the shrimp and eat them on their own or make tacos.

MANGO GREEN TEA POPSICLES

Green tea is a little bit country to mango's rock 'n' roll. When you mix the tea's earthiness with mango's sweet tropicality, though, you get a harmony of flavors that sings on the taste buds. A little zing from lime and creaminess from coconut make these your go-to frozen pops.

MAKES 4

1½ cups frozen mango chunks
1½ cups prepared green tea
¼ cup lime juice
¼ cup coconut cream

SPECIAL EQUIPMENT: popsicle molds

Place the frozen mango, green tea, lime juice, and coconut cream in a blender. Blend until smooth. Pour the mixture into popsicle molds and place in freezer for at least 6 hours, or until fully frozen.

Index

METRIC CONVERSION CHART

Volume Measurements		Weight Measurements		Temperature Conversion	
U.S.	METRIC	U.S.	METRIC	FAHRENHEIT	CELSIUS
1 teaspoon	5 ml	½ ounce	15 g	250	120
1 tablespoon	15 ml	1 ounce	30 g	300	150
¼ cup	60 ml	3 ounces	90 g	325	160
⅓ cup	75 ml	4 ounces	115 g	350	180
½ cup	125 ml	8 ounces	225 g	375	190
⅔ cup	150 ml	12 ounces	350 g	400	200
¾ cup	175 ml	1 pound	450 g	425	220
1 cup	250 ml	2¼ pounds	1 kg	450	230

About the Author

Allyson Reedy is a food writer, restaurant critic, and novelist. Her work has been published in a number of newspapers and magazines, including *The Denver Post* and *Bon Appétit*. She is the author of several cookbooks, including *50 Things to Bake Before You Die* and *The Phone Eats First*. She lives in Denver, Colorado, with her children, husband, and pug.